Haiku

Nine Poems

by Matsuo Basho

Table of Contents

Haiku

What is a haiku?

A haiku is a short, unrhymed poem. It has one stanza (STAN-zuh) of three lines. Haiku poems are often about nature or the seasons. The poems are usually written in the present tense so they seem to be happening as you read them.

What is the purpose of a haiku?

People write haiku poems to capture a moment in time. Haiku poems are like photographs made with words. The idea is to portray, or show, an event or scene in few words. As a result, the poet must choose his or her words very carefully.

People also write haiku poetry to create a strong emotional feeling in the reader, such as happiness, loneliness, or calmness.

How do you read a haiku?

Read each poem as a single sentence or thought. Pause in your reading where you see a comma, dash, or colon. As you read, try to form a picture in your mind of what the poet is seeing, thinking, or describing. Then try to connect the poem to your own life and find a deeper meaning for the haiku.

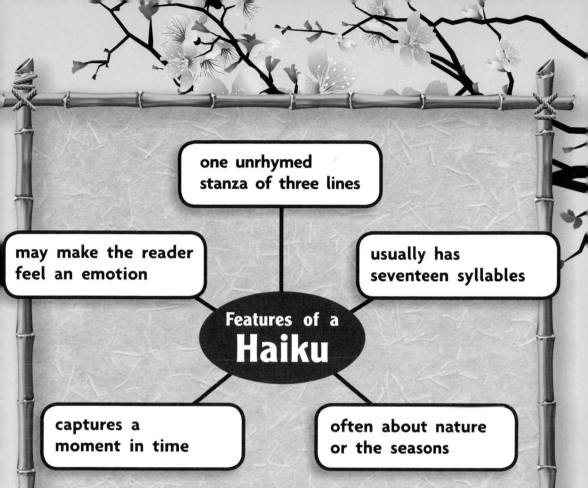

one unrhymed
stanza of three lines

may make the reader
feel an emotion

usually has
seventeen syllables

Features of a
Haiku

captures a
moment in time

often about nature
or the seasons

Who invented haiku?

Haiku is a form of Japanese poetry. It was originally called hokku. At first, people created haiku poems about fun, light topics. Then, in the seventeenth century, serious poets such as Matsuo Basho took haiku to a new level. These poets used haiku to express more meaningful thoughts and feelings and to provide a connection between people and nature.

Structure

A haiku has three lines. The first and third lines have five syllables each. The second line has seven syllables. Here is an example:

The deer's thick brown fur,

the bear's hiding places say

winter is coming.

You will see that some of the poems in this book do not follow the 5-7-5 pattern. That is because the poems were originally written in Japanese and then translated into English. The translators knew it was more important to keep the meaning of the poem rather than the exact syllable count.

Tools Poets Use

Imagery

Haiku writers use words and phrases to make readers think of things they have seen, heard, smelled, tasted, or touched. The mood, or feeling, of the poem depends on whether the memories are good or bad. These words and phrases are examples of imagery, a type of description that creates pictures, or images, in readers' minds. The images help readers understand the poet's ideas by experiencing them with their own senses.

Autumn Haiku

All the field hands

enjoy a noontime nap after

the harvest moon.

All along this road

not a single soul—only

autumn evening comes.

Winter Haiku

Through frozen rice fields

moving slowly on horseback,

my shadow creeps by.

For this lovely bowl

let us arrange these flowers

since there is no rice.

In few words, the poet tells a longer story: There is no rice and his family is hungry, but he tries to look on the bright side by placing some flowers in the bowl to cheer them up.

Chilling winter rains

curtain Mount Fuji, then make it

more beautiful to see.

This haiku captures a snapshot of Mount Fuji on a cold afternoon. By using the word "chilling," the author shows how cold the rain is. The word "curtain" helps readers see the rain veiling the mountain, and then revealing it, making it, somehow, even more beautiful.

Reread the Haiku

Analyze Each Poem
- What is the haiku about?
- What word or words help you create a picture in your mind?
- Reread the second Autumn haiku about the road. This poem might make the reader feel peaceful because no one is really ever alone. There is always nature. Choose one of the other poems and tell what emotion it makes you feel. Then explain your thinking.

Analyze the Tools Poets Use: Imagery
- Reread the first Autumn haiku about the field workers. The poem says that field workers are taking a noontime nap. These words might cause the reader to see people sleeping under trees. Their lunch pails lie on the grass next to them. In the background, a plow sits in the middle of a field. Choose one of the other poems and describe what you see.
- Reread the first Winter haiku about the rice fields. The poet describes the movement of time by including describing words such as "slowly" and "creeps." How do these words create a picture in your mind?

Focus on Words: Word Origins
Make a chart like the one below. Find out where these words come from and then give a definition.

Page	Word	Word Origin	Meaning
6	harvest	Old English: haerfest	time of year for gathering crops
8	shadow		
9	arrange		
10	curtain		

Spring Haiku

1. At the ancient pond

2. a bullfrog plunges into

3. the sound of water.

A haiku follows a strict format. It is an unrhymed stanza of three lines. **The first and third lines have five syllables. The second line has seven syllables.**

A cuckoo cries,

and through a thicket of bamboo

the ⃞late moon⃞ shines.

The poet uses strong imagery to help readers hear the cuckoo's cry. By using the words **late moon**, the poet helps readers picture the moon's brightness as it shines through the dense growth of bamboo trees.

Summer Haiku

The farmer's roadside

hedge provided lunch for

my tired horse.

A haiku captures a moment in time, usually a scene from nature.

Wet with morning dew

and splotched with mud, the melon

looks especially cool.

A haiku draws out emotion. The poet's words help readers draw from their own experiences to not only picture the dew and mud on the melon, but to feel it. Readers can almost taste how cool and refreshing the melon will be, and share in the poet's joy of anticipation.

Reread the Haiku

Analyze Each Poem

- What is the haiku about?
- What word or words help you create a picture in your mind?
- What emotions does it make you feel? Explain your thinking to a partner. Are your emotions the same or different? Explain.

Analyze the Tools Poets Use: Imagery

- Reread the second Summer haiku about the melon. What image comes to mind from the melon being splotched with mud? What image might come to mind if the melon was simply covered in mud? What other word might you use?
- The callout explains the imagery for the second Spring haiku about the cuckoo. Choose one of the other poems and explain the imagery in it. Share your thinking with a partner.

Focus on Words: Word Origins

Make a chart like the one below. Find out where these words come from and then give a definition.

Page	Word	Word Origin	Meaning
12	ancient		
13	thicket		
14	provided		
15	splotched		

Meet the Poet:
Matsuo Basho

Matsuo Basho (1644–1694) was one of the most beloved poets of Japan. His father was a member of the military nobility, but Basho chose a life of wandering and study. His real name was Matsuo Munefusa. He chose the name Basho, which means banana tree, for the tree that grew near the hut where he often went to be alone. In 1667, Basho moved to Edo, which is now Tokyo. There he focused on haiku and helped turn it from playful verse into a serious form of poetry. He continued to travel, too, and used these experiences in his writing. Basho's poetry reflects his love of simplicity and nature and his belief that people should bring their deepest devotion to their work.

How does a poet write a
Haiku?

Reread the first Summer haiku with the horse and think about what Matsuo Basho did to write this poem. How did he develop each line? How can you, as a poet, develop your own haiku?

1. Decide on a Subject

Remember, a haiku captures a particular moment in time. Will you write about:

♦ a particular scene in nature? (examples: a mountain, forest, lake, or group of animals grazing in the fields)
♦ a particular event in nature? (examples: salmon swimming upstream, snow falling, whales jumping out of the water)
♦ your favorite season?
♦ your favorite time of day?

If you have trouble deciding on a subject for your haiku, try one of the following:

♦ Go outside. Take a notebook with you. Use words or sketches to record what you see.
♦ Look at photographs in a nature magazine.
♦ Listen to some pleasing music and write down what it makes you think of.

2. Brainstorm Setting and Plot

Haiku writers ask these questions:

♦ What is my haiku about?
♦ Where does my haiku take place? When?
♦ What is happening in this place?

Brainstorm Imagery

Pretend to "observe" the scene where your haiku takes place. Then create a list of words and phrases that describe the scene and what is happening. Ask yourself:

♦ What moment does my haiku capture?
♦ What words will I use to describe it?
♦ What could I see, hear, smell, taste, and touch if I were there?
♦ How does it make me feel?

Subject	Setting	What happened	Moment	Words	What I see, hear, smell, taste, and touch	How do I feel?
horse	a farmer's roadside hedge, early afternoon in summer	The tired horse eats part of the hedge for its lunch.	A tired horse eating lunch is a common event.	farmer, hedge, lunch, tired, horse	**see:** the horse, the hedge, a farm in the background; **hear:** sounds of the country, including birds, wind blowing, horse munching on the hedge; **smell:** clean grass and air, warm horse flesh; **taste:** my own lunch; **touch:** the horse, the soft hedge, the ground	I feel sorry for the horse because he's so tired. He must have worked hard during the morning hours.

Illustrate Your Thoughts

Before writing your haiku, illustrate what you see. Then use your illustration to help you focus on writing the poem.

Glossary

ancient   (ANE-shent) very old (page 12)

arrange   (uh-RANJE) to place in a particular way (page 9)

curtain   (KER-tun) to cover from view as if with a curtain (page 10)

harvest   (HAR-vest) the time of year when crops are gathered; usually associated with autumn (page 6)

provided   (pruh-VY-ded) made available (page 14)

shadow   (SHA-doh) a dark outline or shape made by objects (page 8)

splotched   (SPLAHCHT) spotted with large, misshaped marks (page 15)

thicket   (THIH-ket) a dense growth of shrubs or trees (page 13)